Jonathan
looks for God

by Regine Schindler
Illustrated by Ursula Verburg

 St Paul Publications

"Mr Spaceman," said Jonathan, "Mr Spaceman, tell me about heaven." The light of the street lamp shone through the window onto the big picture of a spaceman. The spaceman stepped quietly out of the picture, just as he always did when Jonathan could not sleep. He was wearing his thick spacesuit and his huge boots. He sat down on the little table and talked. He talked about rockets. He talked about the moon. He told Jonathan how the earth looked from far away. It was small and round and covered with dots and shone in the light of the sun.

"But what about God?" asked Jonathan. "Have you seen him in heaven?" But the spaceman only laughed. Then he shook his head and stepped slowly back into the picture. Jonathan thought, "He does not want to tell me about God." He was sad. He wanted to know all about God.

The street lamps went off. There were no more lights to be seen in the houses. Everybody was sleeping. But Jonathan went over to the window. He had never seen the sky at night so clearly before. It was quite black, but the stars shone brightly. They were like diamonds sewn onto black velvet. Suddenly Jonathan had an idea. He thought that the night sky was God's cloak. "I must see God's cloak better," he said to himself. "I will go into the garden and try and touch it. I want to see what it feels like."

Jonathan slipped into his boots. Very quietly he unlocked the front door. He crept down the steps outside. He heard the dog growling behind him, but it was only dreaming. As long as it did not wake up and bark Jonathan would be all right! The night was dark and a bit frightening. There were noises that sounded strange and dangerous. Jonathan could hardly see the stars because of the trees and bushes. A ladder was leaning against the tall pear-tree. Jonathan was glad and thought, "If I climb up there I will see the sky much better. Perhaps I can even touch God's cloak."

Jonathan climbed to the top of the ladder. But the starry sky still seemed just as far away. The birds in the tree woke up. They were very excited because they had a visitor in the night. Jonathan sighed, "If I had wings like you I could fly up into the sky, right up to heaven."

But the birds said, "Even we can't fly that high. Our wings are too weak. You should follow the river. You know that a river always starts at the foot of a mountain, so if you find the beginning of the river then you'll find a mountain that you can climb. We're sure the mountain will reach high into the sky, as far as heaven."

"Thank you, kind birds," said Jonathan. "I will look for the mountain."

Jonathan got down from the pear-tree. He left the garden on his own, walked down the dark and lonely streets of the town and found a path that went to the river. It was a lovely night.

He no longer felt scared. He ran as if he was wearing seven league boots. He raced along beside the river and his steps were light and fast. As he followed the river it became smaller and smaller. It turned into a stream, and Jonathan thought, "I'll soon be at the place where the river begins. I'll be where the mountain reaches up high, high into the sky, as far as heaven."

The stars faded slowly away. The sky was no longer black. Jonathan began to see houses and trees, factories and church towers in the light of the dawn. He could hear lorries rattling. A cock crowed. Morning was coming. Jonathan kept on running. He was not a bit tired. The mountain grew bigger and bigger in front of him. He was nearly there.

At the bottom of the mountain there was a little red cable-car. It was going to take things up the mountain. Sacks of potatoes, cases of soft drinks, crates of beer and parcels were being loaded onto it. The two men in peaked caps did not notice Jonathan. He was able to creep in and hide among the many packages.

Soon the sliding doors of the cable-car clanged shut. The little cable-car groaned and creaked as it began to move up the mountain. It was swinging in the air as it moved. Then Jonathan just had to sneeze. He sneezed very loudly. The driver who stood at the controls of the cable-car said: "Is anyone there?"

Jonathan stuck his head out from behind the fat mail bags.

"Well, well, well," said the driver. "And where do you want to go, little man?"

"I want to go right up the mountain. I'm looking for God," answered Jonathan.

"Looking for God, are you? Then I'm not sure you are on the right track. I've not seen him yet."

When the cable-car stopped, Jonathan got out and thanked the driver. The driver smiled and said, "Tell me when you've found God up there."

Jonathan went further up the mountain. He climbed easily, like a goat on a hillside. The ground became steeper and steeper, and rockier and rockier. Jonathan wanted to reach the top of the mountain as soon as he could. From there he was going to climb into heaven.

At last he got to the top. The villages and towns were far away. They looked like tiny toys. Wisps of cloud hung in the air above and below him. And heaven? It seemed even further away than when he was at home. It was still high, high above him. Jonathan was tired, and now he was sad. Tears filled his eyes.

Merry King Wind had been hiding behind a great wall of rock. He saw the little boy and began to blow as hard as he could. Jonathan nearly fell over. Then he was lifted right up into the air. He left the solid ground below and was carried towards the sun and the sky. Jonathan shouted for joy:

"Oh thank you, dear Mr Wind, for being willing to blow me towards heaven."

14

King Wind dropped Jonathan down on a cloud. He sat himself carefully in the middle of the cloud and sailed through the air as if he was riding a big white feather bed. Jonathan called out:

"Tell me, you big soft clouds, have you seen God? Hey, you shining raindrops, do you come from God's watering-can? You, lovely warm sunbeam, what does your path through heaven's roof look like?"

He got no answers. He only heard a distant rumble. It sounded as if everyone who lived in the sky was laughing at him.

The clouds grew blacker and blacker. There was loud thunder. Lightning flashed brighter than the full moon in the night. But Jonathan shouted at the top of his voice:

"Listen lightning, do you come from heaven? Have you seen God?" But the lightning replied:

"None of us has seen God. But we know one thing: God made the sky and the whole of heaven. He is stronger than the heat of the sun. He is faster than merry King Wind. We must all obey him."

Once again kind King Wind took pity on the boy. He was
now sitting on the cloud feeling frightened because of the terrible
thunderstorm that had started. King Wind carried Jonathan
a long way through the air and set him down in a field full of
sweet-smelling flowers.

Jonathan thought that the wind had taken him to a field in
heaven. He turned to a blue flower and said:
"Flower of heaven, surely you know how to reach God."
"My dear little man," answered the flower, "I am not a flower
of heaven but an ordinary bluebell. All I know about God is
that he made me and all the other flowers, in their many, many
colours – red and yellow and violet and blue."
Jonathan looked around him. "Yes, God must be an artist if he
can make so many beautiful flowers."

When Jonathan took a better look around, he saw a house nearby. It was a house with blue shutters, a house with an old pear-tree growing in the garden. A ladder was leaning against the tree. By a window on the ground floor there sat an old dog. Suddenly Jonathan realized that he was back at his own house. And then he said to himself, "That woman coming towards me is my Mummy. The man behind her is my Daddy." He felt warm inside. He was very glad, and he ran to his parents.

Jonathan told them the whole story. He told them about the wonderful night he had had. He told them about the big mountain, about the cable-car and about his flight on the cloud.

"And I've found out something. God is not only up there in heaven."

"Perhaps you are right, Jonathan," said his father. "In the past people used to say: God lives in heaven above. Yet no one has ever seen him. But we can see everything that God has made around us."

And Jonathan cried: "Oh yes, he made the stars and the whole of the sky, the clouds and the lightning and all the beautiful flowers."

"And he made people," his father went on. "He is especially close to people. God does not live up there, somewhere far away from you and me. He also lives with you and me. He lives with everyone. He makes it possible for us to be happy. He makes it possible for us to love each other. He loves all of us."

"And I love you and Mummy as well," said Jonathan. He hugged his father. He carried on thinking. "Yes," he whispered, "you can't see the loving, but you can feel it. It makes us feel warm and happy."

His mother and father took Jonathan by the hand. And Jonathan felt sure, "God is with us now. God knows us. God knows that I am called Jonathan. He loves me just as parents love their children."

That evening Jonathan stood by the window again. He thought, "The sky is not really God's cloak. It's a pity we can't see God." Jonathan was a bit sad.

But he was happy when his mother came to say good-night. "Mummy, I would so like to see God!" he said.

His mother answered, "Then just look at the sky with the silver stars. It belongs to God. You know he made it."

"Yes, it's beautiful," said Jonathan. "God has made beautiful things."

It was very quiet in the room. His mother sat down and Jonathan sat on her lap. He was happy and he thought to himself, "Sometimes we feel God very close to us."

His mother had also been thinking. She said, "I want to tell you something very important about God, Jonathan. God is not a human being. But he can hear as a person does. He hears you. He hears me. He hears everyone. We can talk to him. We can tell him everything." "That's good," said Jonathan. And they prayed together:

> Dear God,
> you made the flowers,
> the stars, the moon, and the big mountain.
> We do not see you,
> but you are with all human beings.
> Help us to feel you close by us every day.
> Thank you for helping us.
> Make us happy with you. Amen.

Notes for parents and teachers

Sometimes children ask us about God. Also we sometimes wish to speak to them of God, thinking perhaps of our baptismal promises. We know that talking about God is an essential element of Christian education. The problem is how to go about it. This little book may be of some help to parents and teachers.

The book does not offer guidelines for a successful discussion, but it tells a story in words and pictures. The child can enter the world of the story's central character, Jonathan. With Jonathan the child can look at the night sky. Like Jonathan, perhaps, he or she will begin to ask questions. With the young hero of the tale, the child can experience all sorts of adventures, which take place partly in the everyday world of children and partly in a fairytale world.

For a child of 7 or 8, these two worlds are equally close. They exist side by side and are in a deep sense equally real. When a young child follows a story, feelings (plain fear or even longings for security or wonder) can become more real than in a very down to earth discussion when, time and again, the child lacks the right words.

In his adventures Jonathan is driven by his persistent questions about God. It is a kind of questioning that is peculiar to small children. It concerns, however, a question that can present itself afresh to adults in the context of this story. It may then become clear to us that we have too often answered the question, to ourselves and our children, with stiff and useless formulae. The main formula of this sort is the one that children frequently carry within themselves as a description of God: God lives in heaven. In Jonathan's eyes this notion of God has the further addition of a cloak. God is therefore a manlike being, though infinitely great and splendid. Jonathan would like to know more about him, and most of all he would like to see him.

It is important that in the course of the story God loses nothing of his greatness and splendour, and similarly that the sky in which Jonathan imagines heaven to be is not debunked as a part of the world in which God is not. The heavens, however, are no longer seen as the dwelling of God. Like the smaller beauties of nature they become part of the creation, a specially impressive part, which can be a symbol for the splendour of God. In this way the child, together with Jonathan, comes to know God the Creator who made all that is. At the same time he or she discovers this in an almost painful way: I cannot see him; he is not a human being.

But Jonathan discovers, and we with him, that one can sense God: he is present in our feelings and our actions, without us being able to describe him or pin him down. The loving relationship of parents and children, as Jonathan experiences it, becomes an image for God; for it involves security and happiness. God is the "Father in heaven", but this heaven is not in competition with the sky of the spaceman, and this heaven does not need to be decorated like a palace of God.

The story ends with a prayer. While the child is introduced to talking to God, to thanking God and petitioning God, he or she can experience God as facing us, as one ready to listen and see to our needs. It is precisely in prayer that God's splendour becomes evident, in a way quite different from the idea of a king in a black velvet cloak at the beginning of the book.

When we speak in this way about God, children and adults both go beyond the need for a particular picture of him, and at the same time they renounce his "usefulness" as an instrument for bringing up children. The formula of an "omnipresent" God who rewards the good and punishes the bad might, in a sense, seem quite useful. But such a God must make children afraid and would tempt adults to a dangerous moral stance. Consequently, in our little book there is no question of this rather widespread style of "using" (or misusing) God. On the contrary, we hope that in this story children who do perhaps fear such a threatening Being will come to know the loving God who one can feel and talk to.

Of course this book is intended to be read and looked at in close contact with a child. It may be useful to read it aloud and look at the pictures several times without forcing a commentary on the child. The reader will then also be attentive to the child's own questions. It is possible that, in doing this, the story may make us feel uncomfortable, because it challenges us to think about our own questions of faith. The end of the book is not meant to be definitive in what it says about God, but rather it aims at being a starting point for discussion, prayer and further story-telling. Later stories may have the experiences of the adult and of the child as their subjects, but biblical stories, showing God's action, can be valuable, and also other tales of people who have experienced God. Other books in this series may be a help.

Original title: *Benjamin sucht den lieben Gott* © 1988 (sixth edition) by Verlag Ernst Kaufmann, Lahr
Translated from the German and adapted for English by Anne Richards and Callan Slipper

St Paul Publications
Middlegreen, Slough SL3 6BT, England
English translation copyright © St Paul Publications 1990
ISBN 085439 307 2
Printed in West Germany

St Paul Publications is an activity of the priests and brothers of the Society of St Paul and
the Daughters of St Paul who proclaim the Gospel through the media of social communication